this
strawberry book
belongs to

Troy Hoover

This book is for
Christopher
Nicholas
Gillian
and
Johnathan.
My favorite little
bears.

Library of Congress Cataloging in Publication Data

Hefter, Richard.
  One bear, two bear.

  "A strawberry book."
  SUMMARY: Zany bears count the numbers from 1 to 10.
  1. Counting—Juvenile literature.   [1. Counting]
I. Title.
QA113.H43   513′.2   80-16544
ISBN: 8374-0951-9

Weekly Reader Books' Edition

one bear
two bears

the strawberry® number book

by Richard Hefter

a strawberry book®

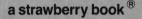

Three bears, four bears;
Through the door bears.

Five bears, six bears;
Do some tricks bears.

Seven bears, eight bears;
Watch the skate bears!

Nine bears, ten bears;
Start again bears.

Ten bears running down the road;
One stops off to watch a toad.

Nine bears charging up the hill;
One bear trips and takes a spill.

Eight bears waiting for a bus;
One decides to hide from us.

Seven bears walking, single file;
One bear wants to rest awhile.

Six bears hopping on one foot;
One of them will just stay put.

Five bears riding on a horse;
One of them falls off, of course.

Four bears left now, playing tag;
One bear finds a sleeping bag.

Three bears sliding down the slope;
One gets tangled in a rope.

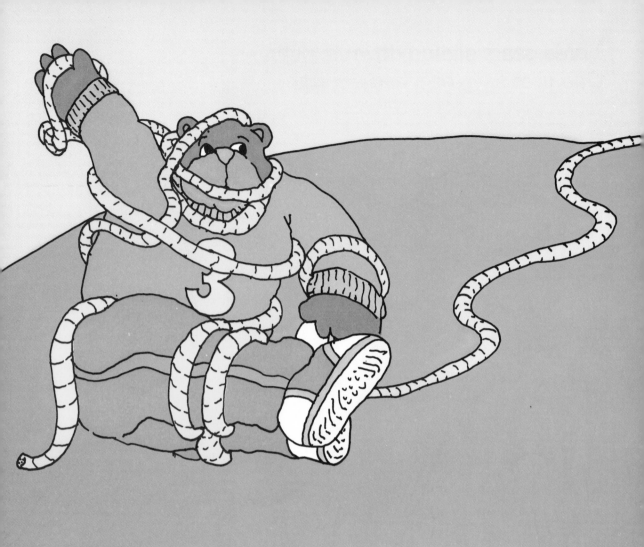

Two bears jogging huff, huff, puff;
One bear says he's had enough.

The last bear left is number one;
He's going home now,
That leaves none.